INVISIBLE LIVES

 **UNIVERSITY OF CALGARY**
Press

INVISIBLE LIVES

CRISTALLE SMITH

Brave & Brilliant Series
ISSN 2371-7238 (Print) ISSN 2371-7246 (Online)

© 2024 Cristalle Smith

University of Calgary Press
2500 University Drive NW
Calgary, Alberta
Canada T2N 1N4
press.ucalgary.ca

All rights reserved.

This book contains discussions of domestic violence and sexual abuse.

No part of this book may be reproduced in any format whatsoever without prior written permission from the publisher, except for brief excerpts quoted in scholarship or review.

This is a work of fiction. Names, characters, businesses, places, events, and incidents are either the products of the author's imagination or used in a fictitious manner. Any resemblance to actual persons, living or dead, or actual events is purely coincidental.

LIBRARY AND ARCHIVES CANADA CATALOGUING IN PUBLICATION

Title: Invisible lives / Cristalle Smith.
Names: Smith, Cristalle, author.
Series: Brave & brilliant series ; no. 38.
Description: Series statement: Brave & brilliant series, 2371-7238 ; no. 38 | Poems.
Identifiers: Canadiana (print) 20240378164 | Canadiana (ebook) 20240378199 | ISBN 9781773855141 (softcover) | ISBN 9781773855134 (hardcover) | ISBN 9781773855165 (EPUB) | ISBN 9781773855158 (PDF)
Subjects: LCGFT: Poetry.
Classification: LCC PS8637.M55965 I58 2024 | DDC C811/.6—dc23

The University of Calgary Press acknowledges the support of the Government of Alberta through the Alberta Media Fund for our publications. We acknowledge the financial support of the Government of Canada. We acknowledge the financial support of the Canada Council for the Arts for our publishing program.

Editing by Helen Hajnoczky
Cover image: Colourbox 45856793
Cover design, page design, and typesetting by Melina Cusano

*To my son Ronin Everett Burbank.
Everything is for you.*

*Special thanks to Matt Rader, Michael V. Smith,
Nancy Holmes, and Margo Tamez. I couldn't be a poet
without your support. I'll remember every lesson well.*

In 2012 my ex-husband tried to choke me to death while I was sleeping.

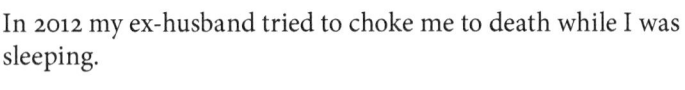

I was 23 years old.

My dreams interrupted.

Flakjacketblitz has signed on.

Submissiveattack: when did you get home from school?

Flakjacketblitz: 10 mins ago, was with steve

Submissiveattack: are you going to joe's birthday this weekend?

Flakjacketblitz is Away right now.

Flakjacketblitz: hey, sry about that my mom wanted me to take out the trash

Submissiveattack: that's alright.

Flakjacketblitz: i might go this weekend, but i have band practice are you going to come over when i record?

It was around the time Jurassic Park was released. My Mom packed me and my two siblings in an old Ford truck with a cab on it. We stuffed our belongings into my new stepfather's 1989 white Toyota van. We put a futon over boxes and headed for the border of Alberta, straight into Montana.

We arrived in Northern Florida. We stayed at my stepdad's brother's house. They had eleven cats. Feces covered floors. Cat hair-fuzzed lasagna on countertops. My step uncle asked us to leave five days after we got there.

We found our first house in the destitution of Newberry, Florida. Across the street from a smoky barbeque pit made from concrete blocks. Sometimes we got pork smothered in heavy sauce. Spicy, sour, sweet. Deep maple pooled in corners of Styrofoam.

An Alligator Bone for Elaine

To My Father's Mother:

Cats and dogs are rain, mist fine
bodies slanting down in cathedral

tune gusts. I have written to offer
what I can find between the bus

stop where you got off and the rosary
they found coiled around your pink

nightgown. Your bones, damp earth
frozen, waiting to turn to summer

mud. Did you arise and go
to the Gulf Stream Isle

of Sanibel; to find briny digits
encapsulating the barb of a horse

shoe crab? Did you see how
they wriggle their legs, like a spider

stuck on its back? I open my mouth,
Grandmother. My teeth pull tight

against freckles. Time is a snowdrift
that laid you down to rest, lichen

inching outward on gypsum, soft
sulfate as I rode my 10 speed past

a wild pack of dogs. I buried
mason jars in the marshlands

near a brown tannin lake. North
America folded on itself. Calgary

to Gainesville. FLA back to AB.
My brother shot BB pellets off

the old stop sign, dreamed he could
hit a squirrel. I visited glass capsules

        sinking in sands and cattails. Tadpole
        pond swallowing a spine in white sun.

Cockroaches scurried over my face. I'd wake, swatting at phantoms in heavy humidity. I slept on moldy green carpets with my little sister. My mother's belly grew round with pregnancy while my stepdad put together a dresser made from carboard boxes we found behind the hardware store on main street.

At school, they kept track of us with clothes pins. On the metal bucket, inside the cafeteria. On our shirt collar, outside on the playground.

Hey girl. Why you wearin' my jeans? Those ain't for you.

She wrapped her arms around my legs, dangling from monkey bars, and yanked.

I crumpled in sandy soil, legs collapsing into heavy sweater. The one I wore for spring days on the prairies.

My mom found a teddy bear at a yard sale. It smelled like old newspapers and stale rain. She opened the bear's side. Velcro gave way to soft silk.

This is where you can put a wind-up clock, when you rest your head against his chest, it's just like a heartbeat.

Call the police, Nick. I see them out there with baseball bats.

Night full of cockroaches and palmetto bugs.

He called 911. I pretended to be asleep. I turned my face towards our makeshift dresser.

Open cardboard sagged in sad rectangles. Socks spilled onto floor. A banana spider held its breath, hanging on a windowpane.

That house across the street. Don't let your little girls out at nighttime.

Armadillo innards melted and dried on hot pavement. The smell followed us past the Piggly Wiggly through the abandoned lot that took us to the library.

I loved to read a series about a girl with a photographic memory. Cam Jansen. Another about a klutzy maid. Amelia Bedelia.

My mom lets us walk alone. We stopped in the Piggly Wiggly sometimes and got sugary drinks in plastic barrels. Liquid burned my throat and stained my mouth purple.

We ate Airheads and teeth rotted under hanging Spanish moss, old oak, and saw palmetto.

About Flakjacketblitz

Whenever you like someone like that, they never like you back.

Submissiveattack: hey lizzie. Did you read Tj's profile?

GnarbroRecords: no, what do you mean?

Submissiveattack: he said, whenever you like someone like that, they never like you back.

GnarbroRecords: oh that's weird.

Submissiveattack: is he talking about you?

GnarbroRecords: no, i mean, I don't think so

Ladybug, Ladybug

My mom's boyfriend Nick. Vietnam vet.
Evolutionary biologist. Zookeeper. Tramp.
Vagrant with a 1989 White Toyota van.

Self-contained ecosystems in mason
jars and kitchen junk. Orange slices
for the ants. Orange peels for the worms.

Stacey lived down the road at the corner
of a curve, where the grass was never
mowed and bent in green bamboo wilts

over cracks in the sidewalk. She had
an early 90s bob, greasy hair plastered
across her speckled forehead. Red

in her freckles. Red in her hair. Her gums
would go red when toothy grins showed
flattened adult teeth in square ends.

Foster care. That's what they told me
it was. And Tracey said, *I never had
a home.* We made one out of boxes

and blankets and Saltine crackers packed
next to teddy bears akimbo. Legs splayed
where the green grass grew and we were lost

in the bamboo forest. I had a bluegreen swim
suit. Pink ruffle trim in criss-crosses over
my shoulder blades. We went to the West

Edmonton Mall. In the waves, with the artificial
flow, I lost sight of her and my toes slipped
off the textured concrete pool. Climbing

up the ladder towards the lifeguard who asked me,
Where is your friend? The first time I felt
fingers inside me was when Stacey came close

to my face and whispered, *Don't worry
this is supposed to feel good.* Her breath
stink washing over me in the hallway

bathroom. It's funny the things you remember.
Brown carpet that smelled like cigarette
butts and looked like the dry remnants

of a riverbed. Drained and baking
in the sun. Stark. Bare lightbulbs
humming in the vanity. White Ivory

Soap that Grandma Jerry used
to make me eat when I swore. *Fuck.
that's what adults do to feel good.*

When you're a girl, you take things into you.
Like breathing chlorine through nostrils,
drowning in recreational wave pools

in February. Like fingers sliding in and out.
Tummy dropping to toes and bluegreen
swimsuits on ankles. That's when you can see

tears on faces near dull vanities
with linoleum countertops curling back
to show particle board from the renovation

of 1978. Legs are shaking, covered
in sweat and she tells me, *That's okay,
I love you anyways.* Sometimes

I wonder how much is in me to cover up
empty aching confusion. Then I remember,
they are always filling me up. To drop me

down. They say their goodbyes
in slow cadence waves, lapping up
bluegreen nylon, spandex.

A ladybug crawls across my fingers.
I capture it in a container poked full
of holes. I hunt aphids

to bring to my carnivorous
beetles in a margarine tub.
I close the lid. They eat them up.

I spilled chicken noodle soup on my lap one rainy afternoon in Airdrie, Alberta.

I was five years old.

Our trailer house had wicker furniture, set against fake wood paneling.

I sat close to the radial dial television screen during lunch time.

       Care Bears was on TV.
              Near boiling soup flowed over bowl.

Cold metal spoon handle.

Liquid poured on my thighs, soaking through neon green bicycle shorts.
I didn't cry as it leaked into white socks, ruffles filled with noodles.

Years later, when I was training to become a lifeguard, I learned that reddened skin indicates a first-degree burn.

A second-degree burn occurs when skin bubbles and blisters.

Never put butter on a burn, the instructor said.

Frag

ments
of

Ficus

Fragments of Ficus

There's a slimy heat in Florida. It covers the world in wetness and weighs down my skin, even when I wear tank tops and have bare feet. Pad on the hot pavement. Sometimes the sun bakes cement until it blisters my flat feet.

Claire Dillard is the name of my teacher. We keep journals and draw the covers. Month by month. There's a theme. Red for February. Green for March. I arrive in her classroom via the roadways of the USA.

Freeway.
    Interstate.
        Highway.
            Tollbooth.

  My stepdad throws coins in the tollbooth's plastic bucket as we near the American South. He's an expert shot. The George Washington quarters circle around with a metallic ring that reminds me of the shopping malls in Alberta where you can send a Looney around a vortex to help kids in hospital.

Light changes. Red to green. *There is a 500 dollar fine for littering.*

        Mrs. Dillard keeps a picture of her husband on her desk. He likes windsailing. He's got grey hair at 54. She's 31.

One day, she takes us on a field trip to the Everglades and hires a guide named Chaulkakeity. Pronounced like this: Chalk-A-Key-Tee.

He draws phonemic pictographs on a whiteboard near some Mac computers that play *Where in the World is Carmen Sandiego?* and *The Oregon Trail.*

Mostly I make pictures on this program called KidPix. And only because of the strange sound effects that come through the speakers when I try to replicate the black and white fuzz on the analogue dial television screen at home.

I like to write in my multicolored journals. Write about snow. Blizzards. Mittens attached by a solitary string across my back and through my sleeves. Get sick from the mosquito bites. Itch my legs. Fingernails always have blood.

Henry Ford invented mass production. And Thomas Edison slept on a cot in his own laboratory. It's still perfectly preserved with a red and yellow quilt. The cot sags in the centre because, the tour guide tells us, Edison slept in there so much.

> Edison did not invent the lightbulb. He improved the filament. That's the difference between invention and innovation.

My mom keeps a wooden plaque up on her wall. She's kept it for years, ever since her health food stores in Calgary and Airdrie shut down. *The doctor of the future will give no medication but will interest his patients in the care of the human frame, diet, and in the cause and prevention of disease~ Thomas Edison.*

Sometimes we live next to a swamp. Sometimes a beach.

Canoes in brackish water. Alligator eyes break surface tension of tannins.

New Jersey. We take planes and automobiles to arrive. Live in the Colts Neck Inn, adjacent to the town where Bruce Springsteen grew up.

> The first story I ever write is about a girl named GiGi. My teacher corrects the spelling (*Gigi or G.G.*, she notes). She submits it to a national writing competition. Tells me with her eyes downcast, *I was sure it was going to win.*

We find an old Victorian in a rough borough. A block from the Karagheusian Rug Mill that Springsteen sings about. A block from a bodega. A block from a triple stabbing. And our place used to be a flop house with 13 full families living inside.

Next my teacher sends me off to compete for a Rotary Scholarship. I wear pink fishnet tights and a t-shirt with Gizmo on it. My competitor, Dionne, rehearses her speech in private and covers the text with her palms in public. Words are secrets.

Eyes behind thick rimmed glasses and aging elegant dinnerware build makeshift walls between me and the uncomfortable shifting bodies in the audience. My poem is awkward as the words land like sloppy soldiers invading the linen-clad tables of the Red Lion Inn.

> Dionne emerges triumphant. A wide smile shows her fine bone teeth. *I talked about*
> *The Matrix.*

Oh, I say.

That night I dream of a girl driving an old Model T through a bumpy prairie pasture. Losing her grip on the steering wheel. Night sky glowing green and freezing above her head. In her nostrils.

I remember it enough to write it down.

I stay up talking. Late at night.

One 3 a.m., Steve tells me how angry he was when he found out that colouring books mixed Triassic dinosaurs with Cretaceous dinosaurs.

Those adults, man. They're always feeding us such fucking bullshit.

Dream at night of numbers, repeating in a helix. Twisting together the tongues of Watson and Crick until their laboratory hopscotch mumbo jumbo crystallizes on the films of Rosalind Franklin. Later, she dies as her cells divide uncontrollably, propagating corrupted DNA.

Miss Havisham and feasts of flesh. A white wedding dress. Restorative. Curative. A dram. A draught. We visit.

I'm sitting with a poet listening to him talk about the scope of written works that engage with human exceptionalism and the demarcation of Nature from City. Rivers covered by concrete beds disappear from our consciousness. Aliens came and planted the glass encased buildings, pushing into the sky. Growing among the square tiles of roads, intersecting near reflective stop signs. A metal crop from Pluto, concrete seeds from Mars. The Periodic Table of Elements is an extraterrestrial farmer's almanac.

Sam Cooke is in my headphones. Sometimes my speakers. Okanagan. Wonder if Plato could sing like that. John Stuart Mill waves his hands in the air like he's the fourth in The Ronettes. Asks the University College London if they'll be his one and only baby.

Let's pretend we were friends. I can bring a bottle of tequila and we can sit quietly and talk. Or not talk at all. Silence fills the holes. Expanding out.

Sentences to interrupt the banality of sadness. Words to corrupt rage. Frost over electrical wires. Flood the ether with rounded sounds from my mouth. Ride out the punctuation until we meet somewhere in the middle.

It'd be the walkway near the Puget Sound. Harbour echoes off the glass art wall. The world would be quiet. Be still. Timbre of glass ringing like a faded bell. All the chapels crumpled on their sides. Sighing wooden buildings. Leaning into forgotten sadness I press into your palm.

      Do you feel it?

      Let's pretend I'd be protected like I was once, 5 years ago sitting on a kitchen floor. Wooden floors and a stone tile cutting board. Inside of a rusty old Dodge truck. Roots and rust digging deep into earth.

Let me be make-believe. Pretend for one night only that we were friends.

I'll sing you this song.

Sinatra on Metal Rivets

Do you know
      what's strange
           about losing
                a connection
                      to a person?

Sometimes there's a phantom pain.

Appendage. A conduit
    in between.

A leg to send love
messages. An arm to hold
the space. Fingers to weave
shadow boxes and necks to bear

      the weight.

Do you know
      in between? I've learned.

There are steps to writing a good poem.
A Canadian poem. A womanly poem.

A poem from the prairies,
from the Rockies
        from the black fly
           cottage swamps
                out East.

Snakes piling up
in Manitoba. Fill a white
plastic bucket with coils.

    let
        them
            slide free.

Here's what I know:

write about Leonard Cohen.

All the deep writer girls
talk about the dark holes
of their belly buttons. Their fingers
running on their tummies. Grab
    a mic and pull
it close. Sinatra on
    metal rivets. And croon
Cohen. Croon it

    long and slow and urging.

Sing about dusty
guitars and men
    gone
        to oil rigs.

Men gone to cowboys. Men gone
to alcohol. Gone to pickup trucks
and waterproof boots. To brothels

    far off from Whyte Avenue.

Gone to Daddy. Gone
To grease. Gone to aching

    longing fucking fighting

to a mistress in a swanky
hotel someplace far away
        like Toronto.

Add seas of golden wheat
swaying under endless prairie skies.

Draw a doodle to hand craft
perfection plastered to a hope chest.

Lacquered to freeze the moment when he says

    he believes in you.

Remember it all enough to write it down.

Think always of missing arms
and legs and hands and necks
holding up faces, familiar
but impossible to recognize.

Play those memories like it's mother
fucking *Groundhog Day* and you're Bill
Murray and you just don't give a fuck.

Master the piano. Let your wrist
jiggle to make some vibrato
on your violin.

Be alone. Always alone.

Watch how the yellow lines
curve along Highway 97

    North. Stop

    your car in Enderby and cry.

Flakjacketblitz: hey girl, u going to the movies tonight?

Submissiveattack: yeah, I was gonna walk from downtown. Maybe go through the cemetery?

Flakjacketblitz: u want company?

Cattails Under the Goodyear Blimp

Precipitation. I'm driving across the border with my stepdad Nick. His white Toyota van from the 1980s replaced by a new red minivan. My double bass in the back. Seats removed. He lets me sleep on the vehicle's carpet. No seat belt. He gets irritable when he's tired or hungry. Or both. I offer to drive. He dozes with his head propped up on a fleece liner from REI.

When you hydroplane, take your foot off the gas and wait for the wheels to gain grip.

Nick's father was a surgeon in Southern Florida, he once sewed up a man with over 120 stab wounds. And before, the Pacific Theatre of War.

When you go into a curve, take your foot off the gas pedal, wait until the centripetal force catches up with you and accelerate after the initial turn.

I hit the back button on the CD player to listen to Hank Williams Sr. wax poetic about that lonesome whippoorwill. Just one more time. I tell myself. Winds come across the prairie. Sway the red vehicle. I travel over the double yellow and correct.

Tap your brakes when you hit ice.

His face is rounded, but still masculine. His skin is tan, and gets tanner when he takes his shirt off in the summertime and complains that he just doesn't like heat that much.

Watch for ice on bridges.

Once fire ants crawled up my legs in the parking lot of Itchetucknee Springs and he grabbed a gallon jug of water and poured it on me. Ants pooled at my feet, their venom swirling ineffectively on the blistering blacktop.

Always assume the other driver isn't paying attention.

My boyfriend of 4 years cheats on me and gets addicted to heroin.

Maybe there's something to be said for the long goodbye. Maybe it's like taking a hit, exhale and prepare.

We hit Sweetgrass, and Nick wonders why the sign says Welcome to Canada/Bienvenue au Canada.

Why isn't that sign in Blackfoot? That's whose territory we are on.

I ask him to tell me about his time as a Lonefighter. Holding a baseball bat in the middle of the night in a corner store in Brocket. The mud eating up his dungarees, plywood on the sides of roads to combat the wet dirt.

Surface runoff. *Agent provocateur.* They're impressed when the phrase rattles off my tongue, and I think of him huddled over in the woods, watching the police throw rocks. Identity covered by black bandanas.

They kicked me out of BYU for wearing a belt made out of rope!

He tells me this as he shows me chords on a guitar. Only 4 chords to play any song. See?

Happy Birthday, to you. Happy Birthday, to you.

Did you know Aura Lee was a song from the Civil War and Elvis turned it into "Love Me Tender?"

He calls my mom a fake hippie poser. A groupie slut bitch.

Groundwater. I'm collecting his stories in quiet, as we listen to *The Chronicles of Narnia* on tape. *The Magician's Nephew.* He hands me a book on the Vietnam War and tells me how recruiters lie through their teeth. Except he wouldn't say a cliché. He wasn't like that.

He writes stories on legal pads. Sometimes a novel. A family hunting mammoths. He reads it to me while my mom is working. He tells me the mechanics of buffalo jumps. Wonders if mammoths could be driven off cliffs. Elephantine bodies covered in fur arcing through the sky above me, crashing down on jagged rocks. Skulls cracked open and children crawling across the bones whitened in the sun.

Transpiration. Evaporation. He shows up to my parent teacher conference, ready to do battle with the burnt out hippie teacher. Nick wears a Spongebob Squarepants character shirt. *What a fucking dick.* He tells me. *No wonder you hate the bastard.* And we watch *The Night of the Living Dead*.

Everything is a story to him. Backpacking through the Superstition Mountains. He kept a gun. Spectres looming in the night, rattling his laboratory containers repurposed for rice and cheese.

Hard cheeses don't need refrigeration, you can take them backpacking. They last for weeks, just sweat a bit.

Condensation. I learn young that my heart aches for no discernible reason. I am often sad. Always alone.

Nick told me he went spelunking. Found a small cave in a hot spring where him and some other grad students bathed on a backpacking trip.

I went into the cave, holding my breath and swam for a bit. I figured I'd make a 180 and return to the entrance. When I turned around, I disturbed the sand from the bottom and couldn't see through the murk.

Swirls of dark sand obstructing his vision, his glasses clutched in his right hand. Like when he taught me how to snorkel off the side of a jetty in Pompano Beach.

You can tell it's a barracuda because its face will be like looking at a coin from the side. Flat edge, body extending out.

Precipitation. I am a girl. I never sleep at night. I make a nest from my blankets and circle around in them until the dawn comes. I can hear the sounds of the trailer house breathing. Later, I am 19 and

I stoke the fire in a potbellied stove in a home with no foundation next to the Salmon River. The doors don't lock and I think of Nick walking in the Arizona wilderness, stumbling across a miner who staked his claim in 1907.

Never show respect to someone who doesn't deserve it.

Loyalty. Fealty. Keep your word. His bamboo shinai clutched in his hand. Judo rolls.

This is how you protect your shoulders and neck.

I hit a deer once, in his brand-new red minivan. The deer jumped into the passenger side door on a winding road on the Idaho side of the Lost Trail Pass. It was summer, the blackness of night closing in around us. I pulled off the road. Nick jumped out into the bush to look for the wounded animal.

He let me cry for 45 minutes without saying anything.

My heart aching for no discernible reason.

Caterwaul

Metal rimmed folds of a boat
cut edges into water. We keep
watermelon on beds of lake weed.

Nylon yellow rope twisting on
alternating green, slicing open
dark seeds. Machetes and bug

juice on a decaying picnic table.
I dream you nightly. A hag
tells me resolutely. Knowing

I don't believe seers. Their crystal
balls rolling across speckled terrazzo
floors. My mother's brew, a swirling

pot of concoctions. Dinosaur dirt
and yucca to dissolve animal waste
in sewage ponds at Hutterite farms

brought on trips to Malaysia. Once I
dreamed you wore corduroy jeans.
Light green swishing. I grabbed

your ankles. They were fine bones
meeting sharp angles and rounded toes.
I think I cried, *Don't leave me*. Something

you would think is cliché. With your film
noir Hong Kong crime mysteries. Black
and white. I took a canoe across salt fresh

waters. In Florida swamps and New Jersey
cranberry bogs there were streams filled
with crushed glass and motor oil. I rubbed

silt across my skin. Metallic mud
Sparkled near stagnant water.

I got a lot of fevers in North Florida.

We left Newberry and moved to Water's Lake.

Our neighbour was a single mom in a defunct trailer house. She must have been 27, with a dated feathered haircut from the 70s.

She was dark-haired Farrah Fawcett, a cigarette hanging from her lips.

She dated a teenaged boy named James from down the road.

He lived in the shed off the side of his family's trailer house.

Once, he took me and my brother inside. A shop vac and metal covered construction lights decorated the unfinished wood room.

He pushed his sleeping bag to the side, cockroaches scattered. He thumbed a black can of Raid, took aim, and sprayed.

Look at those fuckers, he grinned through soft facial hair. *See how they flip over when they're dying?*

Jenny was my best friend at Water's Lake.

> We used to call the radio station and request "I Swear" by All-4-One.

Between rounds of Uno and Rummikub, Jenny told me her uncle was Kevin Bacon. She kept an autographed picture of him in her room.

He was wearing an orange astronaut suit.

Is that from Apollo 13? I asked Jenny one night.

I don't know, she looked to the window. *Hey listen, they're playing "Kissed by the Rose" on the radio.*

James was 15 when he was investigated for burning down dark-haired Farrah Fawcett's house.

My mom said, I think he was jealous.

Jenny lied once. She said I called her fat. I screamed at her from my backyard, my brother got so mad he punched me in the eye.

Quit your fucking bitching, cow.

My legs flipped backwards, tumbling into burrs and crabgrass.

I remember how a black eye feels: shut even when I pressed

open with index finger and thumb.

Carta marina

                    Snakes in my bedsheets, curved on
pillows. Fold back blankets and nesting vipers rattle alarm

clocks at 4:33 AM. Aposematism, keyring in my fist. King Cobra
pulls itself erect and meets me tete-a-tete. That 40 something year

old man appears, greying temples and chops frame consternation.
He pulls snake cheek; tugs scar tissue and a jade finger slides out

on a loop keychain. Silver bells ringing in hand. Serpent mouth
opens wide. Glottis and darkness expand near my eyes. *You took*

my dreams, Emerald King Cobra cries. For a moment,
we are stunned. *Ophiophagus hannah, how we have wronged*

you! Its hood opens like gentle sails catching breeze
above beasts in the *Carta marina*. *Put my dreams back*

into my cheek, King Cobra chides us over glowing forked
tongues. Cobra croons, *You made an island of my brother,*

Aspidochelone; you drowned Capricorn in your constellations;
you silenced Sirens, their lips frothing. I open my keyring. Force

apart circular metal with fingernail. Rotate jade around in loops.
Tinkles
and minces like teeth. I give it back to the man in the middle of his
life.

Before we moved from Water's Lake, Jenny came over to see if I was okay.

        She gave me a crossword puzzle book and neon fabric circles we braided into long
        chains.

You know, my uncle is not Kevin Bacon.

I looked to my feet.

I know Jenny, that's okay.

21 Stunning Hairstyles Perfect for Homecoming

I heard you got some daughters. Remember
your mom had slender feet, blonde hair,

White Keds covering tiny round toes?
As 12-year-olds, we canoed through

green waters listening to Sister Jensen pray
about Last Days, gutters of Salt Lake City

running with blood, admonition for Youths
of Zion, mincing and tinkling as they go.

Sister J said, *King James verse gives words
power to speak water and bread into flesh,*

blood. Summer nights we dreamed
marriages and Melchizedek blessings.

Now you sell Amway, positive cleaning
products to dental hygienists and nurses.

On your birthday, I think
of when we drove from Ogden

to Vancouver in my old green Corolla.
Window smashed, *Care Bear* blanket

tucked in the door, fleece barrier
to sagebrush flats. Bramble turns

to pinky yellow tulips at your wedding
reception. Crinoline presses puffed skirts

up floating ankles and some girls married
in mermaid silhouettes. You preferred

Celestial Glory instead. Crystal Salt Flats
expand white to red desert horizon, cathedral

spires crawling into sky. Mormon temple
teeming with white shoes, white feet.

You wanted to knit me a blanket for old
memories. My sister copy and pasted

from Facebook how your Dad's pickup truck flipped,
your mother's toes uncovered on a hospital bed.

Submissiveattack: i found a picture of a baby otter in this old National Geographic. I cut it out for you.

Flakjacketblitz: lol

Submissiveattack: there was something funny about the way the mom was holding her baby otter that made me think of you

Flakjacketblitz: are u going to the Knitting Factory tonight? I'll drive you to the train station

Submissiveattack: okay, but this time if we go out to eat, you can't not tip the waitress again

Flankjacketblitz: aright, i guess. But don't order a BLT with no bacon and no lettuce. That's just a tomato sandwich.

Submissiveattack: exactly

Excavation of Ponce de León

I'm living where settlers displace the Shoshone. Convergence of the Lemhi River and the River of No Return. Potbellied stove near small hardwood-floored rooms from the 1920s. Perhaps a miner and his family lived here once. Drifting in from Gilmore or Leesburg, places now forgotten in the Bitterroots. Sagebrush knocking against depression newspaper plastered on walls. Tattered gingham curtains swaying against rigid grime in the breeze. Faded in 100 years of sunshine.

They say Sacajawea came from this place. A carved statue of her holding her baby is all that remains. Greeting German tourists at the front of a nature centre with winding gravel paths. Red willow bends and curves near the flowing river, makes a basket out of the land.

A bronze replica of a grizzly bear paws at jumping copper cast salmon. Long since dead to dams.

Signage along the highway to Mud Lake reads about the mercury poisoning of Lewis and Clark. Always Sacajawea immortalized in the National Parks' brown and yellow, pointing West. A destiny manifested.

Annette took me on as her apprentice. Asked me why I should be a midwife. Saw my Great Grandmother holding open her hands in Oyen, Alberta. Catching a baby, wiping off vernix.

And then, gently reclaiming the suffering. Midwife, Undertaker, Mother. Her teleological job title. Even though the living were afraid to handle the new, the old, the dead.

Phone calls in the middle of the night. Most often 3 AM. Full moons are busier.

A round of prenatal, labour and postpartum. Weighing babies in swaddling. Cotton flannel baby scale sling.

One night Annette tells me of dreams. A full, bursting fruit, flowers budding in heavy rains.

And yet another, a woman walks clumsily along a railroad path. Dreams each night of finding a dead calf, half removed from its amniotic sac.

This, she tells me, *is a cord prolapse.*

Place your hand gently on the baby's head. Watch the posterior fontanelle. Push up to allow flow through the umbilical cord. Call 911.

We women, unafraid, stand in the pools of water that come from between our Grandmothers' legs.

Ziploc Goldfish

My mom packed us up into her van in New Jersey, our possessions anchored with a cargo net and bungee cords from Wal-Mart. Blue tarp bubbled over our heads and Mom had to stop every few hours to stop violent flapping in freeway wind. Her hands pulled bungee and net across folded tarp while her face was blank. Hollow of silver grommets.

That's how we grew up. Always

                        on

                                the

                                      run.

1.0

Ponoka. That's where my dad died during deep winter on the Alberta prairies. He was institutionalized full time. Dad believed the Devil lived in his stairway, that the government watched him through cameras in his clothes.

Always check your price tags. That's where they put the implants.

Grandma Geri told me that Dad cried during the day in Ponoka because the doctors took away his bed.

I imagined orderlies hauling the metal bed frame into the hallway of the cuckoo's nest. Clanging against the door frame. Rattling the room.

Don't take away my bed, my father said. *All I have left are my dreams.*

I got the call 45 minutes before my night shift in Pocatello, Idaho. I was 18 years old. My father's body was rotting in a morgue with no refrigeration while his family members debated the finer points of a Catholic memorial set for a Friday.

1.1

I asked the funeral director if I could look at my dad's body.

I drove all night up I-15 North through Montana to reach Alberta. I followed the tire tracks of semis through deep snow. I stopped in Sweetgrass to gas up. I forgot to put on snow boots and wore burgundy Mary Janes with mint green flowers covering my toes. Wet droplets seeped onto my bare skin as the snow melted. I looked at the Red Bulls inside the convenience store. I put my hand to the glass and pulled away.

No, dear. You don't want to see that.

My father changed his name to follow Kabalarian numerology. Don to Damon. Back when he was called Don, he served as a missionary for the Mormon Church in Montreal. Later, he played football in Utah. The square shoulders of his 6'4 frame got broader under pads. A blue and white jersey with 22 across his chest. I keep a picture of him kneeling next to his helmet.

It's stashed in a drawer I never open.

1.2

I was 29 when I found out my dad was sexually abused by Catholic priests when he was a boy. And abused again when he was studying to be a Jesuit.

New Age adages and carob chips in honey sweetened cookies never saved his life. I think my mom tried for salvation.

Instead, we escaped down an alleyway and hid out at a women's shelter near the general hospital in Calgary.

We were gone. I grew up and found drugs hidden in my dad's truck glove box. A Lego brick container with the Smarties logo on the side. A building block escape.

1.3

I was almost 30 when I found out my dad sexually abused my ▇▇▇.
My ▇▇▇ was 4 at the time.

Once, my father drove me and my brother in his white Dodge truck to a graveled area near the Saddledome in Calgary. He reached across me and opened the passenger side door to a group of women.

Do you see these whores? That's what your mother is. A whore. Come here, whore.

I pulled my arms into myself. Looked to the ground, past the fishnet tights and miniskirts. I lifted my eyes up to the group of women.

Get in here. A woman in a red vinyl tank top pursed her lips together. I felt she wanted to reach out and take me from the truck. Her eyes reflected the terror I felt inside. The women backed away from the open passenger side door.

No one said anything over my father's screams.

1.4

I was 14 when I found out my paternal grandmother committed suicide. 25 when someone told me her name.

Elaine.

Sometimes I call my mom to make sure I remember it. I make her say it aloud.

1.5

Memories live in my body. In my muscles. Hiding behind pumping blood. Underneath the electrolytes. Potassium curtain. Magnesium Wizard of Oz.

I felt surging when I pushed my son from my body. I laboured. My husband's hand on my shoulder blade. I slumped over on the bed once my boy was gone from between me. A handprint of blood on my tummy.

1.6

I was 19 when I first tried to take my life.

600 pills.

The paramedics and police found the bottles. They kept the empty pill containers and gave them to the doctors. The nurses counted them up.

It took 1 bottle of Tropicana Orange Juice to get 600 pills down. 45 minutes of gulping and slurping. I played the *Gladiator* soundtrack to help time pass. The song *Now We are Free* on repeat.

1.7

I was 28 when I tried to kill myself again.

I walked in the British Columbia brush. Down a path, overhang of trees. Lay down next to the lake at Sun-Oka Beach. In the dry heat of July.

They tracked my cellphone. Grid coordinates to gritty sand beaches on the grey waters of Okanagan Lake.

I was 4 years old the first time I was sexually molested. 5 when I was raped.

My mother's mother stood over me as I hunched in the corner, cowering under her grandma perfume and baby pink sweater.

That's just something we don't talk about, okay, honey? You know what not to say. The vellus hair on her face stood on end. I could feel the ghost softness of her aging skin.

1.8

Sometimes, when I listen to music, I move my body around. Behind doors shut with locks. Quiet fuzz of headphones. Memories sloshing in my muscles. Drown in the lymphatic fluid stirred up. Running like the Salmon River where I used to sit after a nightlong labour and delivery. Rush of water over rocks. Deep black center.

I go to school and walk between brick walls. Built from the ground up in square puzzle pieces abutting crescent arches. Straight lines, metal crosses, transparent panes.

In my Lego box apartment, I look at the shapes of my father's photographs and letters. He kept them in albums. Once I stripped back the vellum paper to read his correspondence. To cover his pictures with my oily fingerprints.

I couldn't feel my dad breathing from inside the ink.

I pulled at the plastic covering. I tried to touch him when he was in the Canadian Army. He was holding a long gun across his chest. It had a bayonet on the end.

If my dad was alive right now, I'd ask him, *What is the name of that gun, anyways, Dad?*

1.9

I bought mini cinnamon buns from Burger King for my 2-year-old son. He munched on them while he wriggled and screamed in the food court of the Marlborough Mall in Calgary. I sat across the plastic mosaic table and looked at my women's crisis counselor.

You know it only takes a matter of seconds for someone to crush a windpipe? You know that, don't you?

I looked over at my boy. He got up from his seat and tried to run into the flow of pedestrian traffic and shuffling shoes. I restrained him and he wailed. Several people in the food court watched me. Their eyes moving from the papers on the table, to the Burger King wrappers, to my son screaming in my arms.

I stared into the eyes of the crisis counselor. They were soft and brown. Rounded and full. Her Nigerian accent filled my ears. My eyes. My throat.

You know you're lucky to be alive, don't you?

2.0

I was 23 years old when my husband coiled his thick fingers around my throat. I was sleeping. My son tucked in a blue portable crib at the foot of bed. I had been a mother for 2 years. My dad had been dead for 6.

My dad took me to the Calgary Stampede once. Late night lights on carnival games. Goldfish prizes in Ziploc baggies. We rode cars on metal tracks through fun house mirror hallways. Black light paint. Plastic skeleton bones jangling from behind discount store cobwebs.

Sometimes I think of my father's body inside his grey white coffin. How he sang me *Danny Boy* over the phone from Clondalkin, Ireland. How his hand fit over mine on haunted house carnival rides.

I close my eyes and see golden fish sleeping between midway lights.

Sinkhole on Davie BLVD

                        I am a prairie girl gone
from Cowtown. Gone from Stampedes. Hands tingle

electric, purple shock Everglades. Somehow wires
crossed with water pipes under a peach coloured tub.

A local boy tells my sister one night that vultures steal
children away from rust dusted shores of tannin laden

lakes. Suwanee swallowing up commodious gator
tails. We breathe heat. Watch palm fronds transpire

moisture, fix nitrogen to soil. Burrs in crabgrass
attach to socked feet, feckless in the long haul back

to Calgary. Back to whiskey. Back to Hutterite jams
and purple blue fields of flax. We make nests of soft

grey Spanish moss instead of shucking peas at Grandma's
on the prairie. We put nail polish over ticks in our skin,

recognise red yellow rings of the coral snake. In the stables
of Hialeah Park Racetrack, my mother peddles herbal remedies

to trainers before races start. Cigarettes and lips, sucked
between gaunt cheeks, perched on yellow teeth. Mom tells

me all the jockeys subsist on black coffee, cradle
leather whips. And one jockey named Joey Walker

loves my mother, *He told me so*. I dream at night
of thoroughbreds and hammer headed standardbreds,

jiggy joggers out of the gate, jingled coifs covering manes,
clink down grated dirt lanes. Cicada night and thrumming

palmetto bugs, my sister finds a sandhill crane feather.
She fingers pith along hollow bones. *Don't touch*

that! Wash your hands, my mom says. We spot a calico
cat, stretching under an avocado tree, bring her kittens camping

in a damp tent at Manatee Springs. Cottonmouths coil around
green matted algae. My sister whispers, folds her fingers

into my fingers, *Do you think we will ever be home?*

Foil Salvation

You were no Julia
Child. You made your
living from hearty Alberta
stews and perogies over

sour cream and onions. At Oyen, you lived
in the pasture. Gopher prairie girl. Horse
between your thighs. Hutterite jams, whiskey
near the grey grain elevators

of Balzac. We had a trailer house
back when they used to say Airdrie
would connect to Calgary one day.
You bowed to the oven. No apron

on your belly. Tin foil
wrapped earth apples covered
in olive oil. Crisp brown skin.
Sunk my teeth in to pillow soft warmth

and an undercooked crunchy
centre. Baked potato game. You were
a 12-year-old runaway. To a commune
near Mabel Lake. To a campground

in Fernie. To downtown LA.
That bassist asked you to go
out on the road. Maybe
you could have been

famous. By the mirrored
coffee table, you balked
at infantry lines of cocaine
and bricks in a heroin palisade.

Instead, you were a 1970s
Mormon convert. Though never
a Young, Benson, or Smith. Your father
was not Brigham, Ezra, or Joseph.

You were a Dane. A High German
pantomime in the baked potato
parade. But The Saints pushed
their handcarts to their graves.

Wooden spokes turning in mud ruts
past Chimney Rock. Disappearing
under salted meat and abandoned temples
on stolen earth. Old Brigham said, *It is enough.*

This is the right place. Drive on.
In the Salt Lake Valley, they crushed
fine China in brick and mortar
to make the temple spires sparkle

in the sunlight. *The Lord God caused a deep sleep
to fall upon Adam.* You made fried chicken
in a cast iron pan. We called it, *Bread Chicken.*
Because the skin tasted more like the wilt

of a soft baguette dampening in a puddle
near the feet of pigeon in Central Park.
You thought you could lead us to salvation.
We followed you to the Everglades. Pine

Barrens. Salt Flats. Bitterroot
Mountains. We settled in
Lemhi County. No redemption. *The rib
which Lord God had taken from man*

made he a woman. I was sealed
for Time and All Eternity to a boy
with brown curly hair. He brought you

a cord of wood for the stove. He coiled
his thick fingers around my throat. You
said, *Don't call the police. Shut up
and say Amen.* We still have miles

to walk for this tin can crusade.

W. Terminus

It could have been mountains
where ID-28 passed QB beam
plant and local boys had their meth.

Their pot. Their booze. I heard
a toddler drowned in Lemhi River
that summer you went to Fourth

of July Creek and took dirt bikes
to Leesburg. It could have been
the bathtub where I laboured

with my son living inside me
down in Pocatello. How I turned
under the metal faucet and my mom

told me, *Stop moaning, your husband
needs sleep*. It could have been government
maintained hot springs where Bureau of Land

Management workers tried to harness
geothermal heat for radiant concrete.
Change rooms soot black in December

freeze. Gallon jugs to sip in Bitterroot
sulphur. Leave a dollar per person, *Honor
System Please*. In the deep of night, I pull

feather down from my feet, pluck
pillows, build a castle around me. I breathe
you in dreams. It could have been

that you had a certain smell. Unwashed
Carhartt jacket, steel toed boots. Soft face
against your upturned chest. Your hair grew

in a dark V. My hand was small
on your tummy. I slid my foot
into your black dress shoe, one

day as a joke. Size 16 swallowed me.
I left Calgary and took I-15 back to Idaho,
your eyes red in taillights on concrete.

Fix

Fountain Road turns from black ink
to frothy grey in the winter months.
1930s houses lining a side street
to nowhere. I told you about my first

boyfriend TJ who drove a red Jeep
SUV. He wore a silver drum key
on a chain around his neck. Tucked
into his beige Navy t-shirt-hand-me-downs

from his military dad. There was a sleek
green Army sleeping bag stuffed in
TJ's bass drum. Once his hi-hat toppled
over him at a punk rock show. Joe kept it

upright while TJ beat the stacked cymbals
with his foot. Soft leather skateboarder shoes
and a GG Allin patch on his desert camo jacket.
Sex and violence. Oi. Oi. TJ was a Straight

Edge kid who swallowed down oxy
from suburban New Jersey mirrored
medicine cabinets. Last I heard, he got

>	addicted

>	to heroin and punched

a girl in her face. I ride this ghost
wagon with you down Fountain

Road. Other times, I deliver messages to you
in a virtual bottle, blue light restricted on screen
to help me sleep at night. *That's so high school,*
you say. You might be right. 44 year old man

whose hair got greyer. Spreading
from your temples, draining fat from
your cheeks. Mouse brown to steel dust. Turn
this wheel. Tom was half Swedish half

Japanese. An Army nurse who worked
at convalescent homes when he left
the desert. I was 18. Tom was 32. Divorced
2 times. He pinned me down

in the Salt Lake Valley. I cried
on I-15 Idaho. Past Ogden. *Don't be
such a victim*, you scream. You bought me
a battery for my car. Fixed my smashed

taillight. Cracked the dash to access
turn signals. I married a real-life Lennie
Small. Except he was smart. In all
the worst kinds of ways. I taught him

how to read Orwell. He made me
a spice rack from reclaimed wood.
We lived in Missoula, Montana. *I
always wanted to visit there,* you

comment. But I am glad I am
gone.

Repository

Tony's slick black hair
smells like pomade and cologne
when he returns from stints in jail

I call him Daddy. You arrive at Peter
Lougheed Hospital. I travel down
the Deerfoot and find you tucked in a crib.

Calgary, Alberta. 4 February 1990.

You slide wild out between
our mother's thighs. Hit bed
with bounce. Midwife grabbing

tiny hands, emit a small cough. Kef
is the onomatopoeia for bark in French.
I think that's the noise you made.

Gainesville, Florida. 9 July 1994.

I miss the crickets at night, brown
lake lapping sandy shore. Bacterial
overgrowth drops heart rates down

low. Gunmetal scalpels come
to the rescue. I watch *Top Gun*
with a bunch of Mormon kids.

Boca Raton, Florida. 30 December 1996.

Sometimes we ride in a van to no place.
We drive to visit a dying aunt. See family
who can't remember our names. Food fights

in a Chinese restaurant on the side
of Route 9. Enough moments to write.

Quaker Lace

Tea party in celestial spheres. Plastic princess
wands. Click metallic gems on Velcro,

sticking to long hair. Squishy translucent jelly
slippers. Barbie
dolls lounge next to folding swimming pools,

dressed in white lab coats and ballet
shoes permanently stuck to their feet.

It's there

I meet him. Eating up my dreams with jangling
player piano key teeth. Yellow bones rattling
until marrow spills onto a little girl

tea cup set. Hot pink. Lavender flowers
floating in the green ether. Quaker Lace
tablecloth. Pour from the rounded spout

of a swelling pattern tea pot. Here's
what I know. Spindle fibres divide.
Cells build up. Slow twitch fibres release.

There's a blueprint in wolfy eyes.
Beatrix Potter. Bunnies wearing blue jackets.
Geese in bonnets. I'm being held;

listening to his heartbeat. Tucked
on the inside of elbows. My arms
hidden against his chest. Conversation

swallows all the gnosis. *Jane Eyre*
on a Manx beach. Books in binding, thick
pages smell of language. Carries the weight

of heavy black ink. I hear a girl in class
explain how there's a term
for a telepathic connection between two

people. Beyond mere coincidence. *Let me
come in.* Coyote slow trots across the road
bending over vanishing marshlands. Cow-pats

covering the land. Soon they bring orchards instead.
Rows of golden red apples tumbling to the earth
in the Okanagan autumn. Infantry lines scarring

the hillsides. Palmistry of otherworldly
invaders. Tail down, fur canters before the mouth
of a roundabout. Lopes in longer strides, shoulder

stretching under lips and fangs.

Wail II

Boy, I'd write your eulogy. Take
all the broken promises and cut
words until letters jumble, decussate

in a pile on the floor. Crumple up
your mustache. Stuff it in a sticker
box that I repurpose as a first-aid kit.

Dip your glasses in glitter. Cover
up thick black retro frames. Tangle
them in my violin strings. Strange

boy, I'd take your text messages.
iPhone to Android, *I love you*.
Play them on loop over names

you called me. *I've never told
anyone that before*. Your Ma
was somewhere dying, mewls,

Boy, I'd hold you close. You lost
her to IV bags and chemotherapy.
Air comes. First. Cells divide.

Second. Cells malignant. Humming
birds appear. Dancing wings, body
still. Near your visored helmet. GoPro

Boy, I'd sing your censure. Take
my longing and put something
with pens and meaning. Highway

97 North road transmissions. Mabel
Lake. Signage for construction
stops. I am a girl raising

a kid. We ride like we're avenue
warriors. Sojourn with the temperature
gauge. It tilts up. One-man band,

you tom-tom my skin.
Clap. What can be said

of a man who's always dying?
Of a man who's already dead?

Boy, I'd mummify your memories
in soft cotton wraps from my medicine
cabinet. Slather them with witchy salve;

perfume formaldehyde. Tuck
the coffin box away. Under a slab
crawling with ladybugs. You took

my heart. Prince George Boy,
I'll be your strength, you said.
Carry on. Protect me. Off. You left

the lights on once, wailing
in the night hours. Boy,

I'll make a Lite Brite from your
fucking pinewood casket.

A Woman Dreams
After Michael V. Smith

I dream the murder of my body,
there is pain and pressure and
air pushing from lungs
a feeling of

the husband who said he loved me
repeats,
        My hands, my hands. While he sobs little boy tears
onto his
cheeks and into his beard.
        He apparently left his sadness
until now, thinking
I would have been dead on the mattress instead.

I am exhausted, barely present.
   There isn't anything I can ask him.

 My hands, he says,
decidedly, and since
he strikes me as incoherent
and irrational in this moment, I hide.

We have to leave him.

In the weeks that follow, this
seems ridiculous.
I can't remember what it was like
to have someone to drive me and my son around.

I use a red plastic Radio Flyer wagon.
We go to daycare to home to stores,
to nowhere at all.
       One night,
my boy tells me he likes to look at the moon.
I ask him if he wants to grow up to be
        an astronomer.

Yeah, he tells me, white teeth exposed to the winter night air.

Blackness of parking lots and ice-covered pavement.
   Yeah, he tells me,
            Yeah, pizza.

Franky: A Father in Vignettes

My father puts primary colour Christmas bulbs
in his mouth. Holds two in his eyes by furrowing
       his brow.

My mother laughs at the 6'4 flesh Christmas
tree. Bones for branches. Lights for eyes.

My father takes me places in his white
Dodge truck. Tells jokes. Says,

I'm going to Merkelize you, Franky.

Wonder who Franky is. Grabs me
too hard. Tickles my ribs. Some days

he doesn't remember
       to pick me up. Shiny metal gun in his

hand. He visits and we ride the Haunted
Mansion in Disney World. Got a Minnie
Mouse with yellow plastic feet that go click.

Dig my fingernails into his skin
and he brings me close to his World Gym
       tank top. Smells like baby

powder and cologne. *Carnosaur*
in a theatre. I'm six. Puke in the bath

room. Sick from the screams
and dismembered limbs. He takes me

to meet with his professor. Studying English
Lit. Drives some sort of fast car, the kind close
to the ground. Over the railroad bump, 150 km

per hour. He squeals like an infant,
Wasn't that fun, daughter? Let's go

again.

My seat belt is off and I fly up;
suspended animation, a 1980s kid
loose. Knock teeth against the dash. I dreamed

my daddy came back home for me. Waited
near McKnight BLVD NW. Arrives in his big

truck. 3 hours late. He yells out in pain,
        grabs his left arm.
Sails into traffic across Deerfoot Trail. I cry
        and reach for the wheel. *Help me,*

he howls. Green Camry honking
at us head on and it pulls off
into a ditch. My father corrects

the wheel, throws back his head,
laughs. *You should have seen your face,*

Franky, he says.

Wail

Placenta in my hands. Organ of life
red in a kitchen bowl. *Check for missing
chunks*, the midwife says. My thumbs move
over tissue. *They could still be inside her.*

the mother keeps the defunct organ
in a Ziploc bag. Explains, *I'll plant
it after I name my daughter.* Calcified
clumps. Log cabin home. Next birth, her

husband is gone to Alaska. Burning a bonfire
for three days straight to dig a foundation
in the permafrost while she moaned
through back labour and bounced

on a ball. I held my hands
against her. Pelvis rocked
back and forth. Back and forth.

My man is gone to the mountains.

The spokes on his dirt bike wheel. Their silver
tint cracks in lines of sunshine. His bike breaks
through bows of black spruce and defunct pine.
Rocks absorb the mechanical heat. Release

it back in the night. Branches
quivering with fear. He moves
like water over a cliff. Collecting
momentum. Surface runoff-muck

on his brow. A eulogy going 100 km/hour
across the valley bottom. Screaming jaws
widening; my son's head crowns. Second degree
tears through guttural growls. Laboured

for 80 hours. Coming in red cleaves

and animal snarls. He's born without breath.
Lies still. Nurses rub vernix; frantic. Apgar
one. Topsy-turvy boy keeps silent.

Once, I heard the wail of a wildman
captured in a snare. Metal wire
closing around his throat. Gurgling
blood and keening for the dead.

Spirits chasing down his howl.

31 December 1999

1.0

I'm hiding under a dirty mattress in a lopsided trailer house. 2 acres on swampy sand soil, somewhere outside Gainesville. Sometimes I dig my fingers into the earth and they puncture it with ease. Bring back fingernails filled with grit. But now there are wooden slats above my face that create rectangular sections of faded blue material with diamond shaped seams. Yellow carnations and green stems. Musty smell of mold covering the manufactured garden 5 inches from my face.

Maybe it was there, on the dirty linoleum floor, I wished for you. Sometimes I think of where you might have been when I was only a little girl. Hiding from the feral dogs and neighbour boys while I held the VHS cover for *Silence of the Lambs*. I could never figure out why Jodie Foster had a moth on her mouth. I was too afraid to watch and find out. And while I clutched the overexposed portrait of Foster's face, maybe you were walking the streets of Vancouver, wearing some Doc Martens boots, hair going shaggy. Flannel shirts and dark brown corduroy jeans.

2.0

Adventures with women, cosmopolitan and complicated. You told me once of a stewardess. Spending Y2K in Tokyo. I saw you then, wearing a man's silk dressing gown. I thought of you trapped in a mason jar. A child pushing a magnifying glass close to your face and fireworks supplying the light. *I was a kept man*, you told me.

3.0

31 December 1999. Grocery stores cleared out of water bottles. My family rustles on the main floor of the New Jersey Victorian with a porch. In a borough, not a township. Our neighbour's name is Porkchop and his son is Bubba. Carriage house converted to a space for my mom's business. Cardboard barrels full of herbs and spices. Rosehips fragrant next to powdered garlic. I make a pile of blankets on my mom's king bed. She doesn't have a husband, she sleeps alone. I shut the door to keep out the noise.

The numbers are counting down, *The Saint* with Val Kilmer is on. Nuclear fission and asthma. Problems to stop time. 2000 came. Hollowed tiredness in my tummy as I climb the stairs into the attic. Keep the window open to let the chill inside. Burning my face with distant laughter from down the street. It was then, I wished for you again.

Some girls pile on a tire swing in Pompano Beach. Spin it until they get sick. Giggle on the recycled rubber pieces. Jump from monkey bars, arcing through the air with pointed ballerina feet and pink spandex shorts. Climbing above the squares of yellow and black tic-tac-toe. Rotate them faster with their hands. Sleepover to run in the sprinklers that went red from iron in the water.

Trying to sleep on the terrazzo floor. Speckled concrete keeps me cool in the Florida heat. Listening to Deep Blue Something. *And I said what about Breakfast at Tiffany's? She said,* Light cotton sheets. Light cotton blanket. They're stifling me. Roll over next to the box fan and imagine what the turning blades might look like if the light was on.

4.0

On a balcony in Nice. Street cleaners try to sop up heat from the pavement. Clean away the shit. A boy sits across from me, one floor down. White button up shirt halfway open and he presses his fingertips together. We stare at each other for 3 hours. Until my back aches from leaning against wrought iron bars, thick and rectangular. Swill Nyquil on the plane ride home. Nod off while a graduate student studying teenagers rambles about psychology.

I listen to "Roland the Headless Thompson Gunner" four times a day. I see Roland looking for Van Owen and revenge; a ghost holding a machete and cutting down jungle bush. A spectre with an automatic gun. Ra-tat-tat. Raindrops on hurricane shutters. I go with my stepfather to watch waves eat away the shore. Making rivers with tributaries in reverse. A delta leading to the high-rise hotels and abandoned parking lots.

5.0

I wait for you. I am woven into hospital blankets. Tapestry of IV lines, cotton gowns and medical tape. *Roland the Headless Thompson Gunner* in my headphones. I make a mixtape for you with Marianne Faithful and Warren Zevon. You think Randy Newman wrote about werewolves eating up old ladies on the streets of London. *Boy, you're pretty fucking stupid.* My feet hang off the end of the stretcher they keep me on, in a hallway. I'm 6 feet. Jeweled gladiator high heels, straps over open toes, and I'm 3 inches taller than you. At least.

I'm 13 years old. A woman tells me to write a list of everything I want in a man. *It works*, she says. Her daughter got every item. Just. Like. That.

6.0

I look at the blue lines on the white paper. Rectangles running the length of the page. Rip it from my Mead Notebook. Crumple it up in my Trapper Keeper. Put Lisa Frank stickers on my face.

1. Must wear a scarf.

You try to touch the hairs of my cello bow and I push your hand away. *Don't you know that skin oil damages it?*

   2. Must play the drums.

I watch *Escape to Witch Mountain* and the twin girl asks, *If you have everything, then what do you have left to wish for?*

   3. Must have brown hair

My first boyfriend has a flat top. Wears a bullet belt and owns *The Anarchist Cookbook*. Makes napalm in his backyard, 45 minutes outside of New York City. B-list horror movies. And one night I ask him, *Can we watch Silence of the Lambs?* Downloads a copy from LimeWire and he pinches the soft part of my hip. Make it to the end.

4. Must wear glasses.

Skin suits and deep holes in a basement. Clarice Starling feeling around in the dark. Watched by a man with night vision goggles.

7.0

I stare at the VHS cover with Jodie Foster. Me and 3 kids watch *Purple People Eater*. Florida humidity seeps into the lopsided trailer. I bring the VHS outside and we play in the dirt, making a fort from clay sands and large boards of wood. Vic comes home from work and tells us the sand will collapse on one of us and kill us. He says the ambulance wouldn't get here quick enough.

Vic Jr.'s got a lisp and cries at his father. Vic narrows his eyes, *Why the fuck do you have that movie outside in the dirt?*

   5. Must love books.

I'm 6. I plant seeds I got from eating apples. Me and Fraezor steal them from every house on the block. Try to eat them all. 12 Granny Smiths. Sour pucker, crisp crunch. Dig in the ground between landscaped bushes and wood chips. Get a splinter up my nail bed. We write our wishes down on a sheet of paper. Tell ourselves we'll come back in spring and find trees with more fruit falling to the ground on the Alberta prairies.

We walk to Hi Ho and buy penny candies. Drink pop and play Super Mario Brothers at the video game shop. Pay by the minute. Later, Fraze dies in Vernon. Choking on his own vomit. I'm 21.

   7. Must have one syllable name.

8.0

25, then 30. Buffalo Bill collecting insects. I keep the kitchen lights on. Fluorescent bulb humming in the Okanagan night. I got a pinewood desk and a mechanical keyboard. Clicks under my fingers, makes words on a screen. Cursor blinking. Waiting.

Wail III

August 23, 2017

BRITISH COLUMBIA— A relatively unknown filmmaker and editor was found ensconced in a sepulchre of mud in the thick of black spruce below the Coquihalla Summit. Excavators laboured for hours to remove his rigid fingers from the frozen form of a hummingbird, nestled in the palms of his black dirt bike gloves which were clutched to his chest.

It is suspected that the man lost control of his motorcycle when he hit an unexpected patch of blackwater from the Suwanee River. Local authorities were confused by the sudden appearance of the tannin laden liquid. It seems the river broke the time space continuum. Jumping across the continent to take the man down. A rescue boat was sent on the Coldwater River, until the grease from the gears of his white dirt bike sunk the ship. *For those in peril on the sea.* Damp earthen heat permeated the scene. Algae muck from the backs of alligators and manatees preserved the face of the relatively unknown man.

During autopsy, mouth found to contain several cicadas riding palmetto bugs. Outfitted with lances, spears and violins. Prodded by scalpels, the cicadas whisper rush from nightmares and sweep through the trees. They arrive at the ears of a young Kelowna woman who hears them sing every night when she tries to sleep. She can't sleep.

Heart weighed 504 grams. Rapid froth weighed down the ventricles. Latex hands scooped away the mess. The Medical Examiner went out for soup of beef broth noodles. He was said to take half home in a Styrofoam container that looked like a large hot chocolate cup. Later, it was found he had germinated a gelatinous blob.

When the man's boots were removed, a Red Tide washed out from his toes. Sanibel Island seashells swamped fishy guts onto the floor. Police sent the tangle of calcium and bowels to Rum Island Spring where they were accidentally repatriated to a tourist family from Wales. The

Chief of Police turned purple in disgust.

The Medical Examiner noted that the Loop of Henle was replaced by coiled coral snakes. *Red and black, you're safe, Jack. Red and yellow, jump back, Jack.* For some time, the man functioned with a water moccasin as his liver. Kept warm and safe in a bed of Spanish moss.

Ponce de León pronounced the man dead on arrival and fought to have his corpse brought to the Oldest Wooden Schoolhouse in St. Augustine. Weighted down by a rusty sea anchor to stop the hurricane winds from erasing the schoolhouse from the swampy sands.

The girl couldn't be reached for comment, but she was seen tending a patch of sunflowers just below the Arctic Circle holding a copper watering can. Her eyes were clear with sadness and her mouth resolute in loyalty. Her hair lifting, slight, in the breeze. Dancing in the summer winds.

I Have to Sleep at Night with a Telephone in My Hand

Somewhere outside of Oklahoma
we stopped for Pepsi in Styrofoam cups
and burgers in greasy parchment paper.

My brother told me that if I snorted carbonated
drink through double straws my wish might
come true. I hoped for another trailer house

with fake wood paneling down the hallway.
Inhaledon plastic. Hemingway

smacked his lovers to tighten up
his lines. Praise the simplicity
of Hemingway's words. A dog

barked. Rain fell on a telephone pole. *She just
took the beating and did not seek help*, the judge said.

Wilde commented on bloated

red lines of his wife's body after their baby came.
Disgusted the portrait of Dorian Grey. Frown lines

appearing in cracked oil paint. A green light glowing

on a dock across a frothing lake. Fitzgerald might
have taken his words from Zelda. I sniffed at Pepsi
straws. Their double barrel liquid burning the inside

of my sinuses. Watched my older brother double
over in laughter. He was the first man to blacken my eye.
To call me a cunt. My mother screamed, *Call 911*.

He's taking an axe to the front door.

Sometimes I think of uncredited
drugged out Marianne Faithful. Warbling gravel

on a 1980s record. I wonder who taught Mick
Jagger to play. *Cooze.* I remember the first time
I heard that word. In the early 90s, as a young

girl. Tongue slid out between mustachioed lips
and uttered, *What a fucking bitch. You are wicked.*

I remember my ex-husband told
me once I was a sheep. A white

lamb bathing in moonlight.

Six West: Diagnosed with Ehlers Danlos at Kelowna General Hospital

I have become
adept at waiting.   Waiting

for fruit bats to drop
their vampire wings.   Waiting

for yellow jackets
in laundry piles to sting

crosses grey. My grandmother's legs
curve in soft bows. V thighs touch, knees

spread outwards. *Those boys
were never interested in me*,
               she preens.

I have become
what my mother always   feared

I was. A Wikipedia article
reads, *You only have so many*

spoons to spend. Nurse hooks
IV into veins, heart aches

when *Maltese Falcon* plays
on VHS. I visited Thorneycroft DR

in Calgary NW. Hardwood floors
creaking behind rose bushes and sugar

snap peas. Portraits of each grand
daughter, dusted, leaning against

wooden shelves. I asked, *Where*
am I?

Am I talons clipped
around throats, spiraling rotary

phone dial tones? I have become
adept at living in reverse. Night

hours stretched into endless day.

I push myself out of bed. Hips
unsteady, maybe how Grandma felt

at the baseball diamond in 1934
when my grandfather said, *I guess*

heavy set girls look okay. I saw
grey Atlantic waters lapping foreign

stones, tiny red squid stranded
against moss, cement tides   washed

salt clean.

Invisible Lives

Yahoo search bar, Ask Jeeves how
to tell your mom you like simple
curves of a woman's hip. Type

what happens when women don't
love men. Fetch Altavista: what
happens when women don't

kiss men? Women kiss women+
women love women+women don't
love men. My step-father said

my mother was a bull dyke. Butch
bitch, long legs stretching up
and down Fifth Avenue. *Don't you*

*know that with your short haircut
you look just like a man?* LimeWire
downloads *Legend of Billie Jean*. No

men. When I was a girl in Broward
County Florida, heat seeped into speckled
terrazzo floors. I stood in the open

pocket of a fridge door ajar, stuffing
my face with bologna to make pain
go away. That night cicada danced

into crickets and dreamed of hurricane
force winds. Minnie Driver appeared
on TV. Emerald Isle spanning between her

feet. I called the 800 number and requested
brochures, booklets, and cards. *Tour Ireland*,
I sighed. *What's your address?* she asked. 724

NE Second Street or 32 Conover Street or defunct
trailer house 5 minutes from the lake. Calgary
apartment+20 minutes away in Airdrie+New Jersey

red rock playgrounds and black ants. Red
hibiscus bloom in the backyard. I opened
travel books, folded pages back, saw Grafton
Arcade. In my step-grandfather's office
stacked with old National Geographics,
I curled on carpet. Pages huddled by a box

fan, tonal fingers on Nepal, ankles rubbing
whale sharks, wrist veins circling snow
leopards, arctic ice shifts haunting deep.

Some humming drowns out crashing
dishes, slamming doors, screaming
dyke, dyke, dyke, cunt. Cookies contain

search histories. To print papers, hold
Control P: lines of lesbian+lesbian women

love other women. *You little bitch, don't*
you know that no man will ever want you?

Years later, I stood on a ferry
in the Irish Sea, floating towards

Clondalkin and Minnie Driver and green
stretching past me. I jostled secrets,
crossed and uncrossed my legs under

a simple white peasant skirt, never
thinking how my fiancé's large
hand would hold.

Submissiveattack: you there?

Flakjacketblitz: yeah, what's going on

Submissiveattack: do you remember how we always used to talk every night?

Flakjacketblitz: yeah

Submissiveattack: what happened to us anyways?

Flakjacketblitz: i dunno

Flakjacketblitz: i guess some people just never get the lives they wished for, when we were young and all that shit

Lyric Lab Report

Purpose
The purpose of this experiment is to test how fragmented cycles of familial dysfunction are expressed through metaphorical language that enlivens the page with spirit, heart, meaning, resonance. Conditions and results may vary according to elevation and temperature changes.

Questions
How do poetry and lyric language sort trauma into meaningful pieces of discourse? How is meaning constructed through metaphors? What can we learn from sinkholes, cypress knees, golden wheat, and mothering? How can the Suwanee River appear in the Coquihalla Summit?

Hypothesis
1. What I learned from sinkholes is earth swallows up. Water fills

2. slouching caverns, yawning limestone filament.

3. On a boardwalk

4. in Atlantic City, I saw saltwater taffy

5. spin, churning marshmallow lines, pink to light pink to pink. I learned

6. grandmother died in downy drifts, sleeping ice crystals, frost dust eyes.

7. Earth does not rise up to meet bodies, to grow

8. mountains over bones; she yawns, collapses

9. soil on crushed lodgepole pine, sprouts poplar

10. into Spanish moss. Hopeful Monsters ascend

11. punctuated equilibrium, tornado warnings

12. baptise vehicles in ditches, bodies brace

13. terrazzo floors and swampy soils. Land folds

14. over and over. What I learned from sinkholes

15. portals bedrock to cypress knees, Alberta

16. oil pumps listing waves, lurching golden

17. wheat, pelican dines estuary to sea; feeding one and then another, cycles

18. mother to son to daughter.

Experimental Design
University of Idaho is located in a small town near the border of Washington. Moscow, Idaho connects to Pullman, Washington via a highway, some traffic lights, and a Walmart parking lot past the mall.

It was 2011 and I had a job working in a microbiology laboratory for Dr. Hartson. We were doing NIH funded research on cancer. My professor looked at a sequence of DNA in E. Coli that impacted motility. The sequence functioned as an analogue to corrupted DNA cancer cells in animals. Simple. Mess with motility, stop cancer.

I was hired to help with menial tasks. Carting around media, broth, agar plates. Autoclave biohazard bags. Magnetic stir bars in Nalgene plastics. Brew, concoct, swirl. Pour.

Sterilize.

Sometimes I used to think of what would happen if someone shoved me into the autoclave, ala Hansel and Gretel, and I was the witch. No candy cane door handles, just hissing skin melting off flesh.

Heat, pressure, steam.

The woman in charge of the lab was Kasha. She told me she was the first female biochemist in post-War Poland. Or maybe it was *one of the first female biochemists, Cristalle.*

Details like that are gone to me.

But I remember that Kasha's husband was taken as a political prisoner for not toeing a communist line. Or that she once lived in Alberta.

Nabisco flew her someplace like Toronto to consult on the creation of Olestra, the much-anticipated diet-oil of the 90s.

Kasha told those Nabisco guys *something* and moved on. Olestra ended up giving people uncontrollable shits.

Kasha told me lots of things.

Like the time her son lost so much weight he almost died, and she figured it must be because he couldn't digest gluten. *The biochemical process of gluten digestion causes bowel inflammation in all people. It's just that some people can't handle the inflammation.*

Kasha found potatoes and boiled them with salt. *That's how you can eat well, even if you're poor.*

Her husband was released. Her son saved. They left to Canada.

Kasha hated Canadians. She said, *They're all racists. Pretend to be polite to your face, stab you in the back later.*

I told Kasha I was Canadian. *Fine, fine, but Cristalle, stop apologizing for everything.*

Here's something important Kasha told me:

Every scientist in a lab does things a little differently. Watch each one. A preference for a certain pipette tip, a way to organize test-tube racks, which method to move around DNA.

Make a plasmid ring. Put it in the bacteria.

Heat, electricity.

Kasha said, *I don't like to electrocute them. It just feels wrong.*

She told me to pick a scientist and copy them. Scientists are artists. Replicate the methods. Technique. Emulate until mastery.

To remember what you're doing, write it down.

Case Studies
The following Case Studies introduce the overall structure and methods of the experimental design. Case Studies may be followed to produce similar results, but can also be deployed to foster novel scientific discoveries. It is said that Mendelian genetics were found when an ancient bookshelf overturned and a monk's pea plant experiment grew from stoney earth. Purple flowers. Pink flowers.

Red.
    Blue.

A rocket to Pluto.

Case Study A.0223 "Ladybug, Ladybug"
I am thinking of Matt Rader's *Miraculous Hours*, how it impacts my poems. I use Rader's book as a blueprint for how to reflect on childhood experiences with the framing of the sublime. I heard in one of my classes once that the sublime is supposed to fill you with terror. The sublime is an internal manifestation of outside forces.

I want to defamiliarize my familiar memories. I want to create strangeness in landscapes of my childhood. I write trying to emulate *Miraculous Hours*. I then gave drafts to my Artistic and Senior Astronaut Supervisor, Matt Rader.

"Ladybug, Ladybug" came alive when I had a chance to perform it. At the Indigenous Summer Institute, I attended a reading at Woodhaven Eco Centre in Kelowna. We shared food, stories, poems. It was important to recite "Ladybug, Ladybug" with my voice, like the song from my childhood, the song from its title:

Ladybug! Ladybug!
Fly away home.
Your house is on fire.
and your children all gone.
All except one,
and that's little Ann,
for she crept under
the frying pan.

How strange when we sing of little Ann, underneath the frying pan, dance the film *Ladybug, Ladybug* where children suffocate in a refrigerator, hiding from nuclear holocaust.

Case Study C.8920 "Fragments of Ficus"
During the fall of 2017, I had the opportunity to create a lyric essay that explained my poetics. I read Mary Ruefle's *Madness, Rack, and Honey* in preparation. I was also studying with Nancy Holmes in an advanced workshop for my MFA at UBC Okanagan.

I felt free from the constraints of academic verbiage. Ruefle and Holmes inspired me to face my fears and push into them. Poetry is a maze with no ending. A problem with no solution. A space of clashes and uncertainty.

I realized over the last 3 years
      I am okay with uncertainty.

The title of "Fragments of Ficus" is divided into fragments on the page. I wanted words to envelope their own meaning, the layers are an embodied form. I struggled to title this piece for a long time. I had a conversation with my Astronaut Mentor Matt Rader who suggested a title related to Sappho.

Fragments of Sappho, "Fragments of Ficus." See how that works?

I did not want my poetics statement full of vernacular, heavy with the burden of rising yeasty paragraphs, a melon on two tendrils. I meditated on memory until free associations flowed and assembled into Polaroid moments.

I then juxtaposed those moments: Thomas Edison, writing as a young girl, traveling the roads of the United States, the heaviness of Florida. Meaning emerges from the images and sensory information, but also comes from the way the excerpts are compiled. That is to say, meaning comes from between Thomas Edison and a Floridian girlhood. Meaning is as much on the page as it is off the page.

I struggle with form. How should I divide the vignettes? Where do they belong? I try the form of an Encyclopedia, divisions based on academic numbering, simple paragraphs, business paragraphs. Nothing seems to work.

I can see how negative space create pauses in works, slows them down, forces readers to turn the page. I had an "Ah ha!" moment. Jung's golden scarab tap-tapping at the window.

    Let
        Me
            Come
                In.

Case Study Z.0001 "21 Stunning Hairstyles Perfect for Homecoming"

I want to write on the power of experience.

I read many poets. Those poets can tell a story through a mundane object. A pepper that is a hat. A melon that is a baby. A blackberry that is a secret. So fascinating. Compelling.

However, my lived experiences and vulnerabilities are not pepper hats nor melon babies. Not even blackberry secrets.

During my MFA, many things happened to me. I dealt with abuse, physical illness, and personal loss.

A woman who was like a mother to me growing up was in a car accident with her husband. She has been in a vegetative state since the accident. She will be removed from life sustaining support in the coming months.

What more can be said of my surrogate mother? Her small feet hidden under a hospital blanket.

Case Study W.7242 "Invisible Lives"
As Mary Ruefle taught me, I can wear a vase on my head as a hat so my body is an upside down flower.

But even more important than that:

The problem of my poetry. If you are an astronaut or cosmonaut looking for ideas on how to get to space, follow the map of my poem.

Here is the legend:

Tell the whole terrible truth.

Then put the truth into tercets, enjamb the lines, juxtapose the memories. Introduce sensory information. Allow the body to tell the story:

It will be hard. You may cry in your rocket on the way to space. It is then you realize that cosmonaut gloves are not made from fleece.

A downy lining of Neptune. An asteroid belt of upside-down flowers.

But now

the thing is done.

Safety
I came into the lab early each morning. I liked to clean. Dust bookshelves, wipe down lab benches with alcohol, vinegar.

Mix up media, broths. Label vials and tincture bottles on shelves. My own apothecary in Latah County.

Sometimes Kasha came early too.

That morning she was folded over her lab bench. Ashen. Breath laboured.

I could see Kasha was dying in front of me.

I called 911. Comforted her while we waited for the ambulance. Her hand was tiny on my forearm. Soft from age. Light bird bones, fluted hollow fingernails. A phantom nail bed.

They life-flighted her to Spokane. Saved by a heart surgeon.

Kasha recovered 6 weeks later and gave me a present. A card with a note that said she loved me for saving her life. For being at the right place at the right time. She wrote about how no one else was in the building at 6.30 AM and she would have died. They would have found her collapsed on the bench at 9:30 AM when the post-doc came in.

Kasha wrote, *Love you always* at the end of the card. She gifted me one thing: a magnet that says, *No one notices what I do until I don't do it anymore.*

Kasha held me. Her cheeks wet behind her 1970s glasses.

Procedure
I begin with Kasha. She circles my mind. Slight curve of her S back, roundness under beige shirt.

I allow myself to feel everything I know in my body. I recall the sound of her voice, the way her skin felt, the types of clothes she wore in the lab. I think of the way the autoclave smelled after sterilizing a biohazard bag full of media and broth that has gone off. I allow the sensory details to pile up.

It can be an uncomfortable and disorientating experience to visit memories in such vivid details, but this is step one. I let my memories loop until they teach me something new: another image appears, a landscape far-removed from the current one. Two things collapse on each other. I allow my mind to make the associative leaps. There is poetry rising up to subsume memories of Kasha.

Now I work in reverse and ask myself the questions: What is the connection between Kasha and the creation of my poetry? How is Kasha related to my motherhood? How do the sensory details give knowledge?

I try different approaches. I write a paper about Emily Dickinson living in my cupboard; it fails. I write a paper that tries to sound like English literary criticism; it fails. I think of Kasha living in post-War Poland, afraid of the secret police. Her husband is a prisoner and refuses to give up names of his colleagues.

Kasha told me once that they were driven out of Poland a news article ran in her hometown that lauded how Kasha and her husband now worked for a university in Moscow. The journalist did not understand that there was a Moscow, Idaho. It was believed the couple was in Moscow, Russia contributing to the communist cause.

She kept a clipping of the newspaper article because she thought it was so funny. Kasha's girlish giggle rippled the newspaper clipping and she tucked it back into the drawer. We stood together in a microbiology lab near the border of Washington state. How many things had to happen in life for us to be together in that moment?

My lab report incorporates lyricism because the juxtaposition of form is a way to layer on embodied experience. Kasha was a scientist, a scholar, an artist, a mother. I am too a scientist, scholar, artist, and mother. I am all things at once. My poetry is all things at once. It is only though the layering of constituent parts that resonance is achieved.

I have found guidance from poets on the page and in my life.

Michael V. Smith taught me that personal trauma and truth in our writing can be transmitted like a blade wrapped in a blanket. The edges of the cloth are essential to delivering the harshness of the truth. Smith finishes his poetry collection *Bad Ideas* with the poem "A Little Song to Make Sense of the World." Smith writes, "Some truths are so cutting / we need a story // to hold them. Hold them. / Hold them." I hope I crafted a story worthy of holding my truths.

(See results below).

Results
Apollo Aquarium

I loved silver threads, magician scarf
    theatrics in lines of your brow.

Moon is lonely. In the sky

    pastry-wrapped space junk
circles solar powered sails.

  Tea kettle steam erupts, cooling

  engine screech. Plastic orb births

  loose leaf paper. Mechanical pencil

scribe writes Cassiopeia
              across   Mid-Atlantic   night.

   Stars munch crumpets, floss

satellites from teeth. You were machine
   reverbs
caught in super oil novas.

Rusted truck, rusted man's

              throat closed over
              cabaret sounds.

This one's for the boys, for lanterns folded

   in Jupiter

winds, for ethernet cables burrowed
in skin, *Pour one out.*

   Colonists sent to Mars hopscotch
      across red dirt, collect WD-40 rocket

joints. Soft missile pocket retina
shapes:

      seashell Madeleine, UFO
         macaron, llama animal cracker

turns to dust, hourglass mouth
   waterfalls calcium, chalk

at your feet. I loved you

   round pale metallic nettles,
butter bread telescope, dark side moon.

Conclusion
After years of hard work my son and I are planning a road trip across Canada. It is the winter of 2019. We have been living in the Okanagan for 7 years.

Someone told me once that 7 is an auspicious number. I don't know about luck.

But here's what I can tell you:

I am taking my boy to the Royal Tyrel Museum in the Badlands of Drumheller. We will see Hoodoos. Layered red clay. Glacial movements in geologic time.

Jawbones of duck billed dinosaurs and maybe freeze-dried astronaut ice-cream bars.

And poetry—

Poetry is the vehicle that will drive us there.

Bibliography

"A & M Karagheusian." *Wikipedia*, Wikimedia Foundation, 8 Jan. 2024, en.wikipedia.org/wiki/A_%26_M_Karagheusian.

Mikkelson, David. "Thomas Edison on the 'Doctor of the Future.'" *Snopes*, Snopes.com, 25 Jan. 2015, www.snopes.com/fact-check/the-doctor-of-the-future/.

Rader, Matt. *Miraculous Hours*. Nightwood Editions, 2005.

Ruefle, Mary. *Madness, Rack, and Honey*. Wave Books, 2012.

Smith, Michael V. *Bad Ideas*. Nightwood Editions, 2017.

CRISTALLE SMITH has been published in *ARC Poetry*, *CV2*, *subTerrain*, and more. She won the Lush Triumphant Award for Creative Nonfiction in 2020 and has a chapbook with Frog Hollow Press. She lives in Calgary, Alberta, with her son. *Invisible Lives* is her debut poetry collection.

 **BRAVE & BRILLIANT SERIES**

SERIES EDITOR:
Aritha van Herk, Professor, English, University of Calgary
ISSN 2371-7238 (PRINT) ISSN 2371-7246 (ONLINE)

Brave & Brilliant encompasses fiction, poetry, and everything in between and beyond. Bold and lively, each with its own strong and unique voice, Brave & Brilliant books entertain and engage readers with fresh and energetic approaches to storytelling and verse.

No. 1 · *The Book of Sensations* | Sheri-D Wilson
No. 2 · *Throwing the Diamond Hitch* | Emily Ursuliak
No. 3 · *Fail Safe* | Nikki Sheppy
No. 4 · *Quarry* | Tanis Franco
No. 5 · *Visible Cities* | Kathleen Wall and Veronica Geminder
No. 6 · *The Comedian* | Clem Martini
No. 7 · *The High Line Scavenger Hunt* | Lucas Crawford
No. 8 · *Exhibit* | Paul Zits
No. 9 · *Pugg's Portmanteau* | D. M. Bryan
No. 10 · *Dendrite Balconies* | Sean Braune
No. 11 · *The Red Chesterfield* | Wayne Arthurson
No. 12 · *Air Salt* | Ian Kinney
No. 13 · *Legislating Love* | Play by Natalie Meisner, with Director's Notes by Jason Mehmel, and Essays by Kevin Allen and Tereasa Maillie
No. 14 · *The Manhattan Project* | Ken Hunt
No. 15 · *Long Division* | Gil McElroy
No. 16 · *Disappearing in Reverse* | Allie McFarland
No. 17 · *Phillis* | Alison Clarke
No. 18 · *DR SAD* | David Bateman
No. 19 · *Unlocking* | Amy LeBlanc
No. 20 · *Spectral Living* | Andrea King
No. 21 · *Happy Sands* | Barb Howard
No. 22 · *In Singing, He Composed a Song* | Jeremy Stewart
No. 23 · *I Wish I Could be Peter Falk* | Paul Zits
No. 24 · *A Kid Called Chatter* | Chris Kelly
No. 25 · *the book of smaller* | rob mclennan
No. 26 · *An Orchid Astronomy* | Tasnuva Hayden
No. 27 · *Not the Apocalypse I Was Hoping For* | Leslie Greentree
No. 28 · *Refugia* | Patrick Horner
No. 29 · *Five Stalks of Grain* | Adrian Lysenko, Illustrated by Ivanka Theodosia Galadza
No. 30 · *body works* | dennis cooley
No. 31 · *East Grand Lake* | Tim Ryan
No. 32 · *Muster Points* | Lucas Crawford
No. 33 · *Flicker* | Lori Hahnel
No. 34 · *Flight Risk* | A Play by Meg Braem, with Essays by William John Pratt and by David B. Hogan and Philip D. St. John, and Director's Notes by Samantha MacDonald
No. 35 · *The Signs of No* | Judith Pond
No. 36 · *Limited Verse* | David Martin
No. 37 · *We Are Already Ghosts* | Kit Dobson
No. 38 · *Invisible Lives* | Cristalle Smith

www.ingramcontent.com/pod-product-compliance
Lightning Source LLC
Chambersburg PA
CBHW040253170426
43191CB00019B/2399